Life Lessons
from THE INSPIRED WORD of GOD

BOOKS of RUTH and ESTHER

MAX LUCADO
General Editor

Scripture passages taken from:

 The Holy Bible, *New Century Version*

Copyright ©1987, 1988, 1991 by W Publishing Group. All rights reserved.

 The Holy Bible, *New King James Version*

Copyright © 1979, 1980, 1982 by Thomas Nelson. All rights reserved.

All excerpts used by permission.

Design and cover art—by Koechel Peterson and Associates, Inc., Minneapolis, Minnesota.

Produced with the assistance of the Livingstone Corporation.

ISBN: 08499-5246-8
Published By W Publishing Group

TABLE OF CONTENTS

HOW TO STUDY THE BIBLE

BY MAX LUCADO

*T*his is a peculiar book you are holding. Words crafted in another language. Deeds done in a distant era. Events recorded in a far-off land. Counsel offered to a foreign people. This is a peculiar book.

It's surprising that anyone reads it. It's too old. Some of its writings date back five thousand years. It's too bizarre. The book speaks of incredible floods, fires, earthquakes, and people with supernatural abilities. It's too radical. The Bible calls for undying devotion to a carpenter who called himself God's Son.

Logic says this book shouldn't survive. Too old, too bizarre, too radical.

The Bible has been banned, burned, scoffed, and ridiculed. Scholars have mocked it as foolish. Kings have branded it as illegal. A thousand times over it the grave has been dug and the dirge has begun, but somehow the Bible never stays in the grave. Not only has it survived, it has thrived. It is the single most popular book in all of history. It has been the best-selling book in the world for years!

There is no way on earth to explain it. Which perhaps is the only explanation. The answer? The Bible's durability is not found on earth; it is found in heaven. For the millions who have tested its claims and claimed its promises, there is but one answer—the Bible is God's book and God's voice.

As you read it, you would be wise to give some thought to two questions. What is the purpose of the Bible? and How do I study the Bible? Time spent reflecting on these two issues will greatly enhance your Bible study.

What is the purpose of the Bible?

Let the Bible itself answer that question.

Since you were a child you have known the Holy Scriptures which are able to make you wise. And that wisdom leads to salvation through faith in Christ Jesus.

(2 Tim. 3:15)

The purpose of the Bible? Salvation. God's highest passion is to get his children home. His book, the Bible, describes his plan of salvation. The purpose of the Bible is to proclaim God's plan and passion to save his children.

That is the reason this book has endured through the centuries. It dares to tackle the toughest questions about life: Where do I go after I die? Is there a God? What do I do with my fears? The Bible offers answers to these crucial questions. It is the treasure map that leads us to God's highest treasure, eternal life.

But how do we use the Bible? Countless copies of Scripture sit unread on bookshelves and nightstands simply because people don't know how to read it. What can we do to make the Bible real in our lives?

The clearest answer is found in the words of Jesus.

"Ask," he promised, *"and God will give it to you. Search and you will find. Knock, and the door will open for you."*

(Matt. 7:7)

The first step in understanding the Bible is asking God to help us. We should read prayerfully. If anyone understands God's Word, it is because of God and not the reader.

But the Helper will teach you everything and will cause you to remember all that I told you. The Helper is the Holy Spirit whom the Father will send in my name.

(John 14:24)

Before reading the Bible, pray. Invite God to speak to you. Don't go to Scripture looking for your idea, go searching for his.

Not only should we read the Bible prayerfully, we should read it carefully. *Search and you will find* is the pledge. The Bible is not a newspaper to be skimmed but rather a mine to be quarried. *Search for it like silver, and hunt for it like hidden treasure. Then you will understand respect for the LORD, and you will find that you know God* (Prov. 2:4).

Any worthy find requires effort. The Bible is no exception. To understand the Bible you don't have to be brilliant, but you must be willing to roll up your sleeves and search.

Be a worker who is not ashamed and who uses the true teaching in the right way.

(2 Tim. 2:15)

Here's a practical point. Study the Bible a bit at a time. Hunger is not satisfied by eating twenty-one meals in one sitting once a week. The body needs a steady diet to remain strong. So does the soul. When God sent food to his people in the wilderness, he didn't provide loaves already made. Instead, he sent them manna in the shape of *thin flakes, like frost . . . on the desert ground* (Exod. 16:14).

God gave manna in limited portions.

God sends spiritual food the same way. He opens the heavens with just enough nutrients for today's hunger. He provides, *a command here, a command there. A rule here, a rule there. A little lesson here, a little lesson there* (Isa. 28:10).

Don't be discouraged if your reading reaps a small harvest. Some days a lesser portion is all that is needed. What is important is to search every day for that day's message. A steady diet of God's Word over a lifetime builds a healthy soul and mind.

A little girl returned from her first day at school. Her mom asked, "Did you learn anything?" "Apparently not enough," the girl responded, "I have to go back tomorrow and the next day and the next. . . ."

Such is the case with learning. And such is the case with Bible study. Understanding comes little by little over a lifetime.

There is a third step in understanding the Bible. After the asking and seeking comes the knocking. After you ask and search, then knock.

Knock, and the door will open for you.
(Matt. 7:7)

To knock is to stand at God's door. To make yourself available. To climb the steps, cross the porch, stand at the doorway, and volunteer. Knocking goes beyond the realm of thinking and into the realm of acting.

To knock is to ask, What can I do? How can I obey? Where can I go?

It's one thing to know what to do. It's another to do it. But for those who do it, those who choose to obey, a special reward awaits them.

The truly happy are those who carefully study God's perfect law that makes people free, and they continue to study it. They do not forget what they heard, but they obey what God's teaching says. Those who do this will be made happy.

(James 1:25)

What a promise. Happiness comes to those who do what they read! It's the same with medicine. If you only read the label but ignore the pills, it won't help. It's the same with food. If you only read the recipe but never cook, you won't be fed. And it's the same with the Bible. If you only read the words but never obey, you'll never know the joy God has promised.

Ask. Search. Knock. Simple, isn't it? Why don't you give it a try? If you do, you'll see why you are holding the most remarkable book in history.

RUTH

INTRODUCTION

_H_ere is a play with four characters. Character number one is a prostitute.

Character number two is her son. By the time we meet him he is wealthy, powerful, and single. (We wonder if his bachelorhood has anything to do with being the son of a prostitute.)

Character number three is a foreign widow in a clannish culture. Everything about her is different. Speaks with an accent. Wears a different name. Eats different food. Has a different way. Her only friend is her mother-in-law who happens also to be a widow and happens to be:

Character number four. She is older than the first widow. Too old to have kids. When her two sons died and her husband dies, she is left alone. With only a foreigner as a friend.

Four people. Each rejected. Each alone. Four frazzled strings in the bottom of the knitting basket. Left untouched, awaiting the toss of the master-weaver. But he doesn't discard them.

He picks them up and weaves them together.

The result? The unmarried son of the prostitute meets the foreign widow who left her homeland to accompany her mother-in-law. The mother-in-law recognizes the bachelor as a relative and urges her daughter-in-law to make herself available. She does, the two marry, and the single bachelor has a wife—the young widow has a husband, the older widow has a grandson, and we have a story of providential romance.

Such is the story of Ruth.

You'll recognize her as the younger widow. The older is named Naomi. Boaz is the son of the prostitute. And the prostitute? Well, she isn't mentioned in this book. But she is mentioned in, of all places, the Gospel of Matthew.

Read the words in the parentheses of chapter one verse five. Go ahead and flip over there, I'll wait for you.

Did you see it? Salmon was the father of Boaz. (Boaz's mother was Rahab.)

Who would've thought? A harlot on Jesus' family tree.

But these kinds of things happen in the Bible. Aren't we glad they do? Aren't we glad the master-weaver has a place in his plan for each of us?

LESSON ONE

A LOYAL FRIEND

REFLECTION

Begin your study with thoughts on this question.

1. Think of the most loyal person you know. How does that person's loyalty impress you?

_____

_____

_____

BIBLE READING

Read Ruth 1:1–17 from the NCV or the NKJV.

N C V

¹⁻²Long ago when the judges ruled Israel, there was a shortage of food in the land. So a man named Elimelech left the town of Bethlehem in Judah to live in the country of Moab with his wife and his two sons. His wife was named Naomi, and his two sons were named Mahlon and Kilion. They were Ephrathahites from Bethlehem in Judah. When they came to Moab, they settled there.

³Then Naomi's husband, Elimelech, died,

N K J V

¹Now it came to pass, in the days when the judges ruled, that there was a famine in the land. And a certain man of Bethlehem, Judah, went to dwell in the country of Moab, he and his wife and his two sons. ²The name of the man was Elimelech, the name of his wife was Naomi, and the names of his two sons were Mahlon and Chilion—Ephrathites of Bethlehem, Judah. And they went to the country of Moab and remained there. ³Then Elimelech,

and she was left with her two sons. ⁴These sons married women from Moab. One was named Orpah, and the other was named Ruth. Naomi and her sons had lived in Moab about ten years ⁵when Mahlon and Kilion also died. So Naomi was left alone without her husband or her two sons.

⁶While Naomi was in Moab, she heard that the Lord had come to help his people and had given them food again. So she and her daughters-in-law got ready to leave Moab and return home. ⁷Naomi and her daughters-in-law left the place where they had lived and started back to the land of Judah. ⁸But Naomi said to her two daughters-in-law, "Go back home, each of you to your own mother's house. May the Lord be as kind to you as you have been to me and my sons who are now dead. ⁹May the Lord give you another happy home and a new husband."

When Naomi kissed the women good-bye, they began to cry out loud. ¹⁰They said to her, "No, we want to go with you to your people."

¹¹But Naomi said, "My daughters, return to your own homes. Why do you want to go with me? I cannot give birth to more sons to give you new husbands; ¹²go back, my daughters, to your own homes. I am too old to have another husband. Even if I told myself, 'I still have hope' and had another husband tonight, and even if I had more sons, ¹³should you wait until they were grown into men? Should you live for so many years without husbands? Don't do that, my daughters. My life is much too sad for you to share, because the Lord has been against me!"

¹⁴The women cried together out loud again. Then Orpah kissed her mother-in-law Naomi

Naomi's husband, died; and she was left, and her two sons. ⁴Now they took wives of the women of Moab: the name of the one was Orpah, and the name of the other Ruth. And they dwelt there about ten years. ⁵Then both Mahlon and Chilion also died; so the woman survived her two sons and her husband.

⁶Then she arose with her daughters-in-law that she might return from the country of Moab, for she had heard in the country of Moab that the Lord had visited His people by giving them bread. ⁷Therefore she went out from the place where she was, and her two daughters-in-law with her; and they went on the way to return to the land of Judah. ⁸And Naomi said to her two daughters-in-law, "Go, return each to her mother's house. The Lord deal kindly with you, as you have dealt with the dead and with me. ⁹The Lord grant that you may find rest, each in the house of her husband."

So she kissed them, and they lifted up their voices and wept. ¹⁰And they said to her, "Surely we will return with you to your people."

¹¹But Naomi said, "Turn back, my daughters; why will you go with me? Are there still sons in my womb, that they may be your husbands? ¹²Turn back, my daughters, go—for I am too old to have a husband. If I should say I have hope, if I should have a husband tonight and should also bear sons, ¹³would you wait for them till they were grown? Would you restrain yourselves from having husbands? No, my daughters; for it grieves me very much for your sakes that the hand of the Lord has gone out against me!"

¹⁴Then they lifted up their voices and wept

NCV

good-bye, but Ruth held on to her tightly.

¹⁵Naomi said to Ruth, "Look, your sister-in-law is going back to her own people and her own gods. Go back with her."

¹⁶But Ruth said, "Don't beg me to leave you or to stop following you. Where you go, I will go. Where you live, I will live. Your people will be my people, and your God will be my God."

NKJV

again; and Orpah kissed her mother-in-law, but Ruth clung to her.

¹⁵And she said, "Look, your sister-in-law has gone back to her people and to her gods; return after your sister-in-law."

¹⁶But Ruth said:

"Entreat me not to leave you,
Or to turn back from following after you;
For wherever you go, I will go;
And wherever you lodge, I will lodge;
Your people shall be my people,
And your God, my God.
¹⁷ Where you die, I will die,
And there will I be buried.
The LORD do so to me, and more also,
If anything but death parts you and me."

DISCOVERY

Explore the Bible reading by discussing these questions.

2. Explain the turmoil Naomi was probably experiencing because of all that had happened to her.

_____

_____

_____

3. What did Naomi want for her daughters-in-law? What does this reveal about her character?

_____

_____

_____

4. How did Ruth finally convince Naomi of her loyalty?

_____

_____

_____

5. By going to Bethlehem, what would Ruth leave behind?

_____

_____

_____

6. What does Ruth's decision reveal about her character?

_____

_____

_____

INSPIRATION

Here is an uplifting thought from the *Inspirational Study Bible*.

One relationship of this caliber can buoy us through the fiercest storms. It was the Beatles who sang, "Will you still need me, will you still feed me, when I'm sixty-four?" Oh, the agony of being sixty-four (or any age, for that matter) and having no one to care for you or need you. Happy are those who have one companion, one relationship that is not based on looks or performance. Every person is in dire need of at least one faithful friend, or a mate who will look him in the eye and say, "I will never leave you. You may grow old and gray, but I'll never leave you. Your face may wrinkle and your body may ruin, but I'll never leave you. The years may be cruel and the time may be hard, but I'll be here. I will never leave you."

(from *On the Anvil*
by Max Lucado)

RESPONSE

Use these questions to share more deeply with each other.

7. Is it difficult in today's society to be loyal like Ruth? Why?

_____

_____

_____

8. What sacrifices have you made to honor a personal commitment?

_____

_____

_____

9. Think of a person to whom you are committed. How would that person rate your loyalty?

_____

_____

_____

PRAYER

Father, forgive us for the commitments we have broken, the lack of loyalty we have shown, and the people we have hurt. Thank you for your faithfulness, for keeping your promises to us. Give us wisdom and perseverance as we strive to be more loyal in our commitments.

JOURNALING

Take a few moments to record your personal insights from this lesson.

How can I demonstrate loyalty to someone I love?

ADDITIONAL QUESTIONS

10. Why is it important that we be faithful to our commitments in relationships?

_____

_____

_____

11. What blessings have you received from being a faithful friend? A faithful wife or husband? A faithful father or mother?

_____

_____

_____

12. How is Christ a perfect example of loyalty?

_____

_____

_____

For more Bible passages on loyalty to commitments, see Deuteronomy 23:21–23; Hosea 6:3–7; Proverbs 17:17; Matthew 26: 36–46; Luke 9:23-27.

To complete the book of Ruth during this twelve-part study, read Ruth 1:1-22.

ADDITIONAL THOUGHTS

LESSON TWO

ACTS OF KINDNESS

REFLECTION

Begin your study with thoughts on this question.

1. Think of a time when someone was especially kind to you. How did that person's kindness affect your relationship?

_____

_____

_____

BIBLE READING

Read Ruth 2:3–17 from the NCV or the NKJV.

NCV

³So Ruth went to the fields and gathered the grain that the workers cutting the grain had left behind. It just so happened that the field belonged to Boaz, from Elimelech's family.

⁴Soon Boaz came from Bethlehem and greeted his workers, "The LORD be with you!"

And the workers answered, "May the LORD bless you!"

⁵Then Boaz asked his servant in charge of the workers, "Whose girl is that?"

NKJV

³Then she left, and went and gleaned in the field after the reapers. And she happened to come to the part of the field belonging to Boaz, who was of the family of Elimelech.

⁴Now behold, Boaz came from Bethlehem, and said to the reapers, "The LORD be with you!"

And they answered him, "The LORD bless you!"

⁵Then Boaz said to his servant who was in

NCV

[6]The servant answered, "She is the young Moabite woman who came back with Naomi from the country of Moab. [7]She said, 'Please let me follow the workers cutting grain and gather what they leave behind.' She came and has remained here, from morning until just now. She has stopped only a few moments to rest in the shelter."

[8]Then Boaz said to Ruth, "Listen, my daughter. Don't go to gather grain for yourself in another field. Don't even leave this field at all, but continue following closely behind my women workers. [9]Watch to see into which fields they go to cut grain and follow them. I have warned the young men not to bother you. When you are thirsty, you may go and drink from the water jugs that the young men have filled."

[10]Then Ruth bowed low with her face to the ground and said to him, "I am not an Israelite. Why have you been so kind to notice me?"

[11]Boaz answered her, "I know about all the help you have given your mother-in-law after your husband died. You left your father and mother and your own country to come to a nation where you did not know anyone. [12]May the LORD reward you for all you have done. May your wages be paid in full by the LORD, the God of Israel, under whose wings you have come for shelter."

[13]Then Ruth said, "I hope I can continue to please you, sir. You have said kind and encouraging words to me, your servant, though I am not one of your servants."

[14]At mealtime Boaz told Ruth, "Come here. Eat some of our bread and dip it in our sauce." So Ruth sat down beside the workers. Boaz

NKJV

charge of the reapers, "Whose young woman is this?" [6]So the servant who was in charge of the reapers answered and said, "It is the young Moabite woman who came back with Naomi from the country of Moab. [7]And she said, 'Please let me glean and gather after the reapers among the sheaves.' So she came and has continued from morning until now, though she rested a little in the house."

[8]Then Boaz said to Ruth, "You will listen, my daughter, will you not? Do not go to glean in another field, nor go from here, but stay close by my young women. [9]Let your eyes be on the field which they reap, and go after them. Have I not commanded the young men not to touch you? And when you are thirsty, go to the vessels and drink from what the young men have drawn."

[10]So she fell on her face, bowed down to the ground, and said to him, "Why have I found favor in your eyes, that you should take notice of me, since I am a foreigner?"

[11]And Boaz answered and said to her, "It has been fully reported to me, all that you have done for your mother-in-law since the death of your husband, and how you have left your father and your mother and the land of your birth, and have come to a people whom you did not know before. [12]The LORD repay your work, and a full reward be given you by the LORD God of Israel, under whose wings you have come for refuge."

[13]Then she said, "Let me find favor in your sight, my lord; for you have comforted me, and have spoken kindly to your maidservant, though I am not like one of your maidservants."

NCV

handed her some roasted grain, and she ate until she was full; she even had some food left over. [15]When Ruth rose and went back to work, Boaz commanded his workers, "Let her gather even around the piles of cut grain. Don't tell her to go away. [16]In fact, drop some full heads of grain for her from what you have in your hands, and let her gather them. Don't tell her to stop."

[17]So Ruth gathered grain in the field until evening. Then she separated the grain from the chaff, and there was about one-half bushel of barley.

NKJV

[14]Now Boaz said to her at mealtime, "Come here, and eat of the bread, and dip your piece of bread in the vinegar." So she sat beside the reapers, and he passed parched grain to her; and she ate and was satisfied, and kept some back. [15]And when she rose up to glean, Boaz commanded his young men, saying, "Let her glean even among the sheaves, and do not reproach her. [16]Also let grain from the bundles fall purposely for her; leave it that she may glean, and do not rebuke her."

[17]So she gleaned in the field until evening, and beat out what she had gleaned, and it was about an ephah of barley.

DISCOVERY

Explore the Bible reading by discussing these questions.

2. Describe the qualities of Boaz. What kind of person was he?

_____

_____

_____

3. What does the servant's response to Boaz reveal about Ruth?

_____

_____

_____

4. Why did Boaz admire Ruth?

_____

_____

_____

5. In what ways did Boaz show kindness to Ruth?

_____

_____

_____

6. What dangers were present for young women working in the fields?

_____

_____

_____

INSPIRATION

Here is an uplifting thought from the *Inspirational Study Bible.*

Sometimes people think that the only significant things they do are those for which they receive public recognition. Understandably, we all have a fascination with bigness and fame. Sometimes we are deluded into thinking that if we could just have the chance to preach to the hundreds of thousands of people that Billy Graham does we would be doing something worthwhile. We think that in order to do something of ultimate importance we must write the great American novel or paint some artistic masterpiece. There is a common notion that significance in life depends on some kind of public recognition. But such is not the case. Really gratifying deeds are often done quietly and with hardly any recognition. . . .

Some of the most important things we do in life are often neither dramatic nor memorable. Happily, on Judgment Day, Jesus will reward a lot of people who hardly remember the important things for which they will be honored. Sending a card of appreciation to someone who is a bit down and needs a lift, visiting a shut-in who is lonely, baby-sitting for a harried mother who needs a few hours off, calling someone on the phone to show that you care, and giving a glass of cool water in the name of Christ are not the sorts of things that we even remember doing after they are done. But the people we do them for often remember, and I know that Jesus never forgets.

(from *Who Switched the Price Tags?*
by Tony Campolo)

RESPONSE

Use these questions to share more deeply with each other.

7. What character attributes did Ruth exhibit?

_____

_____

_____

8. How did Ruth experience God's faithfulness?

_____

_____

_____

9. How has God recently shown his faithfulness and provided for your needs?

_____

_____

_____

PRAYER

Father, you have richly blessed us in so many ways. Thank you for providing exactly what we need and so much more. Show us how we can be kind to others, and give us a generous heart to share what we have been given.

JOURNALING

Take a few moments to record your personal insights from this lesson.

What small acts of kindness can I do to brighten someone's day?

ADDITIONAL QUESTIONS

10. What kinds of work in today's society parallel the work of gleaning?

_____

_____

_____

11. Why is kindness important in developing Christian character?

_____

_____

_____

12. How can you help someone in need?

_____

_____

_____

For more Bible passages on acts of kindness, see 1 Samuel 20; Matthew 9:18–26; 26:6–13; Luke 1:29–41.

To complete the book of Ruth during this twelve-part study, read Ruth 2:1–23.

LESSON THREE

TAKING RISKS

REFLECTION

Begin your study with thoughts on this question.

1. Have you ever risked your good reputation for a person or cause? Explain.

_____

_____

_____

BIBLE READING

Read Ruth 3:1–15 from the NCV or the NKJV.

N C V

¹Then Naomi, Ruth's mother-in-law, said to her, "My daughter, I must find a suitable home for you, one that will be good for you. ²Now Boaz, whose young women you worked with, is our close relative. Tonight he will be working at the threshing floor. ³Wash yourself, put on perfume, change your clothes, and go down to the threshing floor. But don't let him know you're there until he has finished his dinner. ⁴Watch him so you will know where he lies down to

N K J V

¹Then Naomi her mother-in-law said to her, "My daughter, shall I not seek security for you, that it may be well with you? ²Now Boaz, whose young women you were with, is he not our relative? In fact, he is winnowing barley tonight at the threshing floor. ³Therefore wash yourself and anoint yourself, put on your best garment and go down to the threshing floor; but do not make yourself known to the man until he has finished eating and drinking. ⁴Then it shall be,

NCV

sleep. When he lies down, go and lift the cover off his feet and lie down. He will tell you what you should do."

⁵Then Ruth answered, "I will do everything you say."

⁶So Ruth went down to the threshing floor and did all her mother-in-law told her to do. ⁷After his evening meal, Boaz felt good and went to sleep lying beside the pile of grain. Ruth went to him quietly and lifted the cover from his feet and lay down.

⁸About midnight Boaz was startled and rolled over. There was a woman lying near his feet! ⁹Boaz asked, "Who are you?"

She said, "I am Ruth, your servant girl. Spread your cover over me, because you are a relative who is supposed to take care of me."

¹⁰Then Boaz said, "The LORD bless you, my daughter. This act of kindness is greater than the kindness you showed to Naomi in the beginning. You didn't look for a young man to marry, either rich or poor. ¹¹Now, my daughter, don't be afraid. I will do everything you ask, because all the people in our town know you are a good woman. ¹²It is true that I am a relative who is to take care of you, but you have a closer relative than I. ¹³Stay here tonight, and in the morning we will see if he will take care of you. If he decides to take care of you, that is fine. But if he refuses, I will take care of you myself, as surely as the LORD lives. So stay here until morning."

¹⁴So Ruth stayed near his feet until morning but got up while it was still too dark to recognize anyone. Boaz thought, "People in town must not know that the woman came here to

NKJV

when he lies down, that you shall notice the place where he lies; and you shall go in, uncover his feet, and lie down; and he will tell you what you should do."

⁵And she said to her, "All that you say to me I will do."

⁶So she went down to the threshing floor and did according to all that her mother-in-law instructed her. ⁷And after Boaz had eaten and drunk, and his heart was cheerful, he went to lie down at the end of the heap of grain; and she came softly, uncovered his feet, and lay down.

⁸Now it happened at midnight that the man was startled, and turned himself; and there, a woman was lying at his feet. ⁹And he said, "Who are you?"

So she answered, "I am Ruth, your maidservant. Take your maidservant under your wing, for you are a close relative."

¹⁰Then he said, "Blessed are you of the LORD, my daughter! For you have shown more kindness at the end than at the beginning, in that you did not go after young men, whether poor or rich. ¹¹And now, my daughter, do not fear. I will do for you all that you request, for all the people of my town know that you are a virtuous woman. ¹²Now it is true that I am a close relative; however, there is a relative closer than I. ¹³Stay this night, and in the morning it shall be that if he will perform the duty of a close relative for you—good; let him do it. But if he does not want to perform the duty for you, then I will perform the duty for you, as the LORD lives! Lie down until morning."

¹⁴So she lay at his feet until morning, and she arose before one could recognize another.

NCV	NKJV
the threshing floor." ¹⁵So Boaz said to Ruth, "Bring me your shawl and hold it open." So Ruth held her shawl open, and Boaz poured six portions of barley into it. Boaz then put it on her head and went back to the city.	Then he said, "Do not let it be known that the woman came to the threshing floor." ¹⁵Also he said, "Bring the shawl that is on you and hold it." And when she held it, he measured six ephahs of barley, and laid it on her. Then she went into the city.

DISCOVERY

Explore the Bible reading by discussing these questions.

2. What did Naomi encourage Ruth to do?

_____

_____

_____

3. What risk was Ruth taking by going to Boaz?

_____

_____

_____

4. How did Boaz react when he discovered Ruth at his feet?

_____

_____

_____

5. What does Boaz's reaction reveal about his character?

_____

_____

_____

6. In what ways did Boaz take a risk?

_____

_____

_____

INSPIRATION

Here is an uplifting thought from the *Inspirational Study Bible.*

It is true that there are great possibilities for failure [when taking risks] and, if you fail, there will be those who will mock you. But mockers are not important. Those who like to point when the risk-takers stumble don't count. The criticisms of those who sit back, observe, and offer smug suggestions can be discounted. The Promised Land belongs to the person who takes the risks, whose face is marred with dust and sweat, who strives valiantly while daring everything, who may err and fall, but who has done his or her best. This person's place shall never be with those cold and timid souls who know neither victory nor defeat.

Oh, if only I could persuade timid souls I meet to listen to that inner voice of the Spirit, which challenges us to attempt great things for God and expect great things from God. Oh, if only I could inspire them to heed that inner urging that tells them "Go for it!" I cannot say what a person should do with life, but I can say what a person should not do with it. No one should devote one's life to safety, to a course of action that offers no challenge and no fun.

(from *Who Switched the Price Tags?*
by Tony Campolo)

RESPONSE

Use these questions to share more deeply with each other.

7. What can we learn from Ruth's willingness to follow Naomi's plan?

_____

_____

_____

8. What admirable character traits do you see in Ruth?

_____

_____

_____

9. What character trait would you like to cultivate in your own life? How?

_____

_____

_____

PRAYER

Father, sometimes you ask us to step out in faith and that can bring anxiety. Forgive us when we lack the faith to take that risk. Please give us the courage to trust you and to obey.

JOURNALING

Take a few moments to record your personal insights from this lesson.

How can I trust in God's plan when the way ahead is uncertain?

ADDITIONAL QUESTIONS

10. What are some of the costs of obeying God today?

_____

_____

_____

11. What personal sacrifices have you made to obey God?

_____

_____

_____

12. What blessings have you enjoyed because of your obedience?

_____

_____

_____

For more Bible passages on trusting obedience, see Genesis 12:1–5; 22:1–19; Luke 3; Acts 20:17–24.

To complete the book of Ruth during this twelve-part study, read Ruth 3:1–18.

ADDITIONAL THOUGHTS

LESSON FOUR

KEEPING INTEGRITY

REFLECTION

Begin your study with thoughts on this question.

1. Have you ever taken a shortcut that hurt you? Explain.

_____

_____

_____

BIBLE READING

Read Ruth 4:1–13 from the NCV or the NKJV.

N C V

¹Boaz went to the city gate and sat there until the close relative he had mentioned passed by. Boaz called to him, "Come here, friend, and sit down." So the man came over and sat down. ²Boaz gathered ten of the older leaders of the city and told them, "Sit down here!" So they sat down.

³Then Boaz said to the close relative, "Naomi, who has come back from the country of Moab, wants to sell the piece of land that belonged to our relative Elimelech. ⁴So I decided to tell you about it: If you want to buy

N K J V

¹Now Boaz went up to the gate and sat down there; and behold, the close relative of whom Boaz had spoken came by. So Boaz said, "Come aside, friend, sit down here." So he came aside and sat down. ²And he took ten men of the elders of the city, and said, "Sit down here." So they sat down. ³Then he said to the close relative, "Naomi, who has come back from the country of Moab, sold the piece of land which belonged to our brother Elimelech. ⁴And I thought to inform you, saying, 'Buy it back in the presence of the inhabitants and the elders

NCV

back the land, then buy it in front of the people who are sitting here and in front of the older leaders of my people. But if you don't want to buy it, tell me, because you are the only one who can buy it, and I am next after you."

The close relative answered, "I will buy back the land."

⁵Then Boaz explained, "When you buy the land from Naomi, you must also marry Ruth, the Moabite, the dead man's wife. That way, the land will stay in the dead man's name."

⁶The close relative answered, "I can't buy back the land. If I did, I might harm what I can pass on to my own sons. I cannot buy the land back, so buy it yourself."

⁷Long ago in Israel when people traded or bought back something, one person took off his sandal and gave it to the other person. This was the proof of ownership in Israel.

⁸So the close relative said to Boaz, "Buy the land yourself," and he took off his sandal.

⁹Then Boaz said to the older leaders and to all the people, "You are witnesses today. I am buying from Naomi everything that belonged to Elimelech and Kilion and Mahlon. ¹⁰I am also taking Ruth, the Moabite who was the wife of Mahlon, as my wife. I am doing this so her dead husband's property will stay in his name and his name will not be separated from his family and his hometown. You are witnesses today."

¹¹So all the people and older leaders who were at the city gate said, "We are witnesses. May the LORD make this woman, who is coming into your home, like Rachel and Leah, who had many children and built up the people of

NKJV

of my people. If you will redeem it, redeem it; but if you will not redeem it, then tell me, that I may know; for there is no one but you to redeem it, and I am next after you.'"

And he said, "I will redeem it."

⁵Then Boaz said, "On the day you buy the field from the hand of Naomi, you must also buy it from Ruth the Moabitess, the wife of the dead, to perpetuate the name of the dead through his inheritance."

⁶And the close relative said, "I cannot redeem it for myself, lest I ruin my own inheritance. You redeem my right of redemption for yourself, for I cannot redeem it."

⁷Now this was the custom in former times in Israel concerning redeeming and exchanging, to confirm anything: one man took off his sandal and gave it to the other, and this was a confirmation in Israel.

⁸Therefore the close relative said to Boaz, "Buy it for yourself." So he took off his sandal.

⁹And Boaz said to the elders and all the people, "You are witnesses this day that I have bought all that was Elimelech's, and all that was Chilion's and Mahlon's, from the hand of Naomi. ¹⁰Moreover, Ruth the Moabitess, the widow of Mahlon, I have acquired as my wife, to perpetuate the name of the dead through his inheritance, that the name of the dead may not be cut off from among his brethren and from his position at the gate. You are witnesses this day."

¹¹And all the people who were at the gate, and the elders, said, "We are witnesses. The LORD make the woman who is coming to your house like Rachel and Leah, the two who built

NCV

Israel. May you become powerful in the district of Ephrathah and famous in Bethlehem. ¹²As Tamar gave birth to Judah's son Perez, may the LORD give you many children through Ruth. May your family be great like his."

¹³So Boaz took Ruth home as his wife and had sexual relations with her. The LORD let her become pregnant, and she gave birth to a son.

NKJV

the house of Israel; and may you prosper in Ephrathah and be famous in Bethlehem. ¹²May your house be like the house of Perez, whom Tamar bore to Judah, because of the offspring which the LORD will give you from this young woman."

¹³So Boaz took Ruth and she became his wife; and when he went in to her, the LORD gave her conception, and she bore a son.

DISCOVERY

Explore the Bible reading by discussing these questions.

2. Who did Boaz invite to witness his negotiation with his relative?

_____

_____

_____

3. How did Boaz show his respect for his closest relative? for Ruth? for Ruth's first husband?

_____

_____

_____

4. What personal sacrifices was Boaz willing to make to do what was right?

_____

_____

5. How was the people's blessing on Boaz and Ruth fulfilled?

_____

_____

_____

6. List evidence from this passage that Boaz was a man of integrity.

_____

_____

_____

INSPIRATION

Here is an uplifting thought from the *Inspirational Study Bible*.

Now for the sake of a few idealistic souls who could assume only the best and think, I can hardly wait to live like this; this is going to be fun! I want to bring you back ever so gently to reality. When you decide to live like Christ among the selfish and strong-willed, God will honor your decision, but . . . you will encounter misunderstanding and mistreatment. You will be taken advantage of. However, don't make another wrong assumption by thinking that if you are going through tough times, you are off target. Not so. Doing what is right is never a stroll through a rose garden. Jesus' plan for living may be simple, but it is not easy. . . .

No matter how painful it may be, let us trust Him to bring good from our living His way.

The Lord Jesus Christ is the model to follow—and you remember where He wound up! But think of all those who were once His enemies, now His friends. You and I would certainly be numbered among them. The force of love is absolutely unconquerable.

(from *Simple Faith*
by Chuck Swindoll)

RESPONSE

Use these questions to share more deeply with each other.

7. What lessons can we learn from Boaz about dealing with people?

_____

_____

_____

8. When have you seen someone stand up for what is right? How did that person's example affect you?

_____

_____

_____

9. How can you stand up for what is right at work? at home? at church?

_____

_____

_____

PRAYER

Dear God, forgive us when we do not fully trust you and try to do things our own way. Continually remind us that your way is best. Guide us as we make decisions and prompt us to do what is right.

JOURNALING

Take a few moments to record your personal insights from this lesson.

How can I be faithful to do what is right and trust God with the outcome?

ADDITIONAL QUESTIONS

10. For what reasons do people compromise their integrity?

_____

_____

_____

11. In what circumstances is it difficult for you to do what is right?

_____

_____

_____

12. How can you better equip yourself to deal with those circumstances in the future?

_____

_____

_____

For more Bible passages on honorable dealings, see Genesis 39:6–12; 1 Samuel 1; 1 Kings 3:16–28; Psalm 25:21.

To complete the book of Ruth during this twelve-part study, read Ruth 4:1–22.

ADDITIONAL THOUGHTS

ESTHER

INTRODUCTION

*T*he Book of Esther. Some things about it you love. Some things you admire. But there is one thing about it that leaves you scratching your head.

You love the story. A Jewish girl raised in Persia by a cousin named Mordecai. She becomes the wife of the king by winning the Miss Persia contest. Her husband is Xerxes. (Better known to some as Ahasuerus, which sounds like something you do when you have a bad cold.)

It's a rags-to-riches romance, though you've got to wonder how much romance could occur when you are married to a guy who could chop your head off if you popped into his office without an appointment. But that's what Esther did. She took the chance at the chance it would save her nation.

That is the part of Esther you admire. Aside from being a beauty, she was gutsy. Xerxes's right-hand man is Haman. (A name that, as you'll soon see, sounds curiously close to "hangman.") Haman was a raging Nazi. Nothing would suit him better than annihilation of the Jews. One day he got his chance. Mordecai, Esther's foster father, refused to bow before Haman. Haman was so mad he convinced Xerxes to let him do away with the whole nation.

That's where Esther comes in. Literally. She comes into the king's chambers uninvited but not unprepared. After getting the Jews to pray and fast for three days, she puts on her royal robes and stands at the door. Xerxes likes what he sees and invites her in. One invitation leads to another, and by the time she finishes, Xerxes not only agrees to call off the massacre but orders Haman to hang from the same gallows Haman had built for Mordecai.

Whew! Quite a lady, this Esther. You have to admire her courage. You have to love her story. But there is one thing that is tough to figure. God's name never appears in the entire book. His actions do. His thoughts do. His plan does. His fingerprints are on every page. But his name never appears. Could it be that God is more concerned about getting the job done than getting credit?

LESSON FIVE

BE PREPARED

REFLECTION

Begin your study with thoughts on this question.

1. Can you look back on your life and see how God prepared you for the tasks he gave you? Explain.

_____

_____

_____

BIBLE READING

Read Esther 2:1–13 from the NCV or the NKJV.

NCV

¹Later, when King Xerxes was not so angry, he remembered Vashti and what she had done and his order about her. ²Then the king's personal servants suggested, "Let a search be made for beautiful young girls for the king. ³Let the king choose supervisors in every state of his kingdom to bring every beautiful young girl

NKJV

¹After these things, when the wrath of King Ahasuerus subsided, he remembered Vashti, what she had done, and what had been decreed against her. ²Then the king's servants who attended him said: "Let beautiful young virgins be sought for the king; ³and let the king appoint officers in all the provinces of his kingdom,

NCV

to the palace at Susa. They should be taken to the women's quarters and put under the care of Hegai, the king's eunuch in charge of the women. And let beauty treatments be given to them. ⁴Then let the girl who most pleases the king become queen in place of Vashti." The king liked this idea, so he did as they said.

⁵Now there was a Jewish man in the palace of Susa whose name was Mordecai son of Jair. Jair was the son of Shimei, the son of Kish. Mordecai was from the tribe of Benjamin, ⁶which had been taken captive from Jerusalem by Nebuchadnezzar king of Babylon. They were part of the group taken into captivity with Jehoiachin king of Judah. ⁷Mordecai had a cousin named Hadassah, who had no father or mother, so Mordecai took care of her. Hadassah was also called Esther, and she had a very pretty figure and face. Mordecai had adopted her as his own daughter when her father and mother died.

⁸When the king's command and order had been heard, many girls had been brought to the palace in Susa and put under the care of Hegai. Esther was also taken to the king's palace and put under the care of Hegai, who was in charge of the women. ⁹Esther pleased Hegai, and he liked her. So Hegai quickly began giving Esther her beauty treatments and special food. He gave her seven servant girls chosen from the king's palace. Then he moved her and her seven servant girls to the best part of the women's quarters.

¹⁰Esther did not tell anyone about her family or who her people were, because Mordecai had told her not to. ¹¹Every day Mordecai walked

NKJV

that they may gather all the beautiful young virgins to Shushan the citadel, into the women's quarters, under the custody of Hegai the king's eunuch, custodian of the women. And let beauty preparations be given them. ⁴Then let the young woman who pleases the king be queen instead of Vashti."

This thing pleased the king, and he did so.

⁵In Shushan the citadel there was a certain Jew whose name was Mordecai the son of Jair, the son of Shimei, the son of Kish, a Benjamite. ⁶Kish had been carried away from Jerusalem with the captives who had been captured with Jeconiah king of Judah, whom Nebuchadnezzar the king of Babylon had carried away. ⁷And Mordecai had brought up Hadassah, that is, Esther, his uncle's daughter, for she had neither father nor mother. The young woman was lovely and beautiful. When her father and mother died, Mordecai took her as his own daughter.

⁸So it was, when the king's command and decree were heard, and when many young women were gathered at Shushan the citadel, under the custody of Hegai, that Esther also was taken to the king's palace, into the care of Hegai the custodian of the women. ⁹Now the young woman pleased him, and she obtained his favor; so he readily gave beauty preparations to her, besides her allowance. Then seven choice maidservants were provided for her from the king's palace, and he moved her and her maidservants to the best place in the house of the women.

¹⁰Esther had not revealed her people or family, for Mordecai had charged her not to reveal

NCV

back and forth near the courtyard where the king's women lived to find out how Esther was and what was happening to her.

[12]Before a girl could take her turn with King Xerxes, she had to complete twelve months of beauty treatments that were ordered for the women. For six months she was treated with oil and myrrh and for six months with perfumes and cosmetics. [13]Then she was ready to go to the king. Anything she asked for was given to her to take with her from the women's quarters to the king's palace.

NKJV

it. [11]And every day Mordecai paced in front of the court of the women's quarters, to learn of Esther's welfare and what was happening to her.

[12]Each young woman's turn came to go in to King Ahasuerus after she had completed twelve months' preparation, according to the regulations for the women, for thus were the days of their preparation apportioned: six months with oil of myrrh, and six months with perfumes and preparations for beautifying women. [13]Thus prepared, each young woman went to the king, and she was given whatever she desired to take with her from the women's quarters to the king's palace.

DISCOVERY

Explore the Bible reading by discussing these questions.

2. Why was a search made for all the beautiful young girls?

_____

_____

_____

3. What preparations did the girls make before meeting the king?

_____

_____

_____

4. How is Esther's physical appearance described in the passage?

_____

_____

_____

5. What did Esther receive because Hegai was pleased with her?

_____

_____

_____

6. What is known about Esther's family history?

_____

_____

_____

INSPIRATION

Here is an uplifting thought from the *Inspirational Study Bible.*

God is economical. He doesn't waste training or experience. He knows what we are doing, what we are learning, and how he is going to use all of that five, ten, twenty years from now.

It's easy to be disappointed when we have prepared for "the plan of God for my life," only to have the door shut in our faces.

That's because we were busy focusing on the plan when God was focusing on the preparation. Watch how he uses that preparation in a whole new way.

When the signals are blurred and you are uncertain, keep on praying, getting Christian counsel, but don't stop what you are doing. Trust him to steer you if you are on the wrong course. But don't stop!

A sailboat's rudder is useless while the sails are down. Set sail, get going. You can't get any direction until the wind fills the sails. Then when the wind changes, be ready to come about. God may have to change your course, but when he does, you will have the momentum for it.

God knows how to move you when the time comes for you to be moved. He knows what is happening to you and what should be happening for you. In other words, trust God to be God. There isn't anything he doesn't know.

(from *God Guides Your Tomorrows*
by Roger C. Palms)

RESPONSE

Use these questions to share more deeply with each other.

7. How do Mordecai's actions reveal his concern for Esther?

_____

_____

_____

8. List some practical ways God prepares us for future tasks.

_____

_____

_____

9. What can you do to be better prepared for what God has for you?

_____

_____

_____

PRAYER

Father, we are comforted knowing that you have a master plan for each of us. Give us discipline to spend daily time with you and prepare us for what our future holds.

JOURNALING

Take a few moments to record your personal insights from this lesson.

How is God preparing me for the future?

ADDITIONAL QUESTIONS

10. How can we demonstrate faith in God in the midst of uncertainty?

_____

_____

_____

11. What can you do if you are unsure of God's plan for you?

_____

_____

_____

12. How can you use your talents and abilities to serve God today?

_____

_____

_____

For more Bible passages on preparation, see Numbers 28:1–8; Matthew 24:36–51; 1 Peter 3:15–16

To complete the book of Esther during this twelve-part study, read Esther 1:1–2:23.

ADDITIONAL THOUGHTS

LESSON SIX

STANDING FIRM

REFLECTION

Begin your study with thoughts on this question.

1. Think of a time when you stood up for your beliefs. How did that affect you?

_____

_____

_____

BIBLE READING

Read Esther 3:1–11 from the NCV or the NKJV.

NCV

¹After these things happened, King Xerxes honored Haman son of Hammedatha the Agagite. He gave him a new rank that was higher than all the important men. ²All the royal officers at the king's gate would bow down and kneel before Haman, as the king had ordered. But Mordecai would not bow down or show him honor.

³Then the royal officers at the king's gate asked Mordecai, "Why don't you obey the king's command?" ⁴And they said this to him every

NKJV

¹After these things King Ahasuerus promoted Haman, the son of Hammedatha the Agagite, and advanced him and set his seat above all the princes who were with him. ²And all the king's servants who were within the king's gate bowed and paid homage to Haman, for so the king had commanded concerning him. But Mordecai would not bow or pay homage. ³Then the king's servants who were within the king's gate said to Mordecai, "Why do you transgress the king's command?" ⁴Now it

NCV

day. When he did not listen to them, they told Haman about it. They wanted to see if Haman would accept Mordecai's behavior because Mordecai had told them he was Jewish.

⁵When Haman saw that Mordecai would not bow down to him or honor him, he became very angry. ⁶He thought of himself as too important to try to kill only Mordecai. He had been told who the people of Mordecai were, so he looked for a way to destroy all of Mordecai's people, the Jews, in all of Xerxes' kingdom.

⁷It was in the first month of the twelfth year of King Xerxes' rule—the month of Nisan. Pur (that is, the lot) was thrown before Haman to choose a day and a month. So the twelfth month, the month of Adar, was chosen.

⁸Then Haman said to King Xerxes, "There is a certain group of people scattered among the other people in all the states of your kingdom. Their customs are different from those of all the other people, and they do not obey the king's laws. It is not right for you to allow them to continue living in your kingdom. ⁹If it pleases the king, let an order be given to destroy those people. Then I will pay seven hundred fifty thousand pounds of silver to those who do the king's business, and they will put it into the royal treasury."

¹⁰So the king took his signet ring off and gave it to Haman son of Hammedatha, the Agagite, the enemy of the Jewish people. ¹¹Then the king said to Haman, "The money and the people are yours. Do with them as you please."

NKJV

happened, when they spoke to him daily and he would not listen to them, that they told it to Haman, to see whether Mordecai's words would stand; for Mordecai had told them that he was a Jew. ⁵When Haman saw that Mordecai did not bow or pay him homage, Haman was filled with wrath. ⁶But he disdained to lay hands on Mordecai alone, for they had told him of the people of Mordecai. Instead, Haman sought to destroy all the Jews who were throughout the whole kingdom of Ahasuerus—the people of Mordecai.

⁷In the first month, which is the month of Nisan, in the twelfth year of King Ahasuerus, they cast Pur (that is, the lot), before Haman to determine the day and the month, until it fell on the twelfth month, which is the month of Adar.

⁸Then Haman said to King Ahasuerus, "There is a certain people scattered and dispersed among the people in all the provinces of your kingdom; their laws are different from all other people's, and they do not keep the king's laws. Therefore it is not fitting for the king to let them remain. ⁹If it pleases the king, let a decree be written that they be destroyed, and I will pay ten thousand talents of silver into the hands of those who do the work, to bring it into the king's treasuries."

¹⁰So the king took his signet ring from his hand and gave it to Haman, the son of Hammedatha the Agagite, the enemy of the Jews. ¹¹And the king said to Haman, "The money and the people are given to you, to do with them as seems good to you."

DISCOVERY

Explore the Bible reading by discussing these questions.

2. What did Mordecai refuse to do?

_____

_____

_____

3. Why did the royal officers at the king's gate tell Haman about Mordecai's behavior?

_____

_____

_____

4. What was Haman's response to Mordecai's refusal to bow down to him?

_____

_____

_____

5. How did Haman use his authority to punish Mordecai?

_____

_____

_____

6. What character qualities did Mordecai demonstrate?

_____

_____

_____

INSPIRATION

Here is an uplifting thought from the *Inspirational Study Bible.*

We shall all feel very much ashamed if we do not yield to Jesus on the point He has asked us to yield to Him. Paul says—"My determination is to be my utmost for His highest." To get there is a question of will, not of debate nor of reasoning, but a surrender of will, an absolute and irrevocable surrender on that point. An overweening consideration for ourselves is the thing that keeps us from that decision, though we put it that we are considering others. When we consider what it will cost others if we obey the call of Jesus, we tell God He does not know what our obedience will mean. Keep to the point; He does know. Shut out every other consideration and keep yourself before God for this one thing only—My Utmost for His Highest. I am determined to be absolutely and entirely for Him and for Him alone. . . .

God's order has to work up to a crisis in our lives because we will not heed the gentler way. He brings us to the place where He asks us to be our utmost for Him, and we begin to debate; then He produces a providential crisis where we have to decide—for or against, and from that point the "Great Divide" begins.

If the crisis has come to you on any line, surrender your will to Him absolutely and irrevocably.

(from *My Utmost for His Highest* by Oswald Chambers)

RESPONSE

Use these questions to share more deeply with each other.

7. What can we learn from this passage about standing firm in our beliefs?

   _____

   _____

   _____

8. How does the world pressure us to compromise our convictions?

   _____

   _____

   _____

9. What have you had to risk or give up to stay true to your convictions?

   _____

   _____

   _____

PRAYER

Dear Father, so often we are weak when we should be strong. Thank you for giving us your strength, for replacing defeat with victory. Strengthen us to be loyal despite any embarrassment or persecution that faces us.

JOURNALING

Take a few moments to record your personal insights from this lesson.

How has God helped me to be strong in my faith?

ADDITIONAL QUESTIONS

10. Why are Christians harassed and persecuted for their beliefs?

_____

_____

_____

11. Why do we sometimes waver about our beliefs when we feel intimated?

_____

_____

_____

12. How can you better prepare yourself to stand up for your beliefs, in spite of pressure or persecution?

_____

_____

_____

For more Bible passages on standing firm, see Joshua 24:15; Psalm 33:11; 125:1; Matthew 7:24, 25.

To complete the book of Esther during this twelve-part study, read Esther 3:1–15.

ADDITIONAL THOUGHTS

LESSON SEVEN

RESPONSIBILITY

REFLECTION

Begin your study with thoughts on this question.

1. Think of a time when you struggled to do what was right. What was the outcome? How did that affect you?

_____

_____

_____

BIBLE READING

Read Esther 4:1–17 from the NCV or the NKJV.

NCV

¹When Mordecai heard about all that had been done, he tore his clothes, put on rough cloth and ashes, and went out into the city crying loudly and painfully. ²But Mordecai went only as far as the king's gate, because no one was allowed to enter that gate dressed in rough cloth. ³As the king's order reached every area, there was great sadness and loud crying among the Jewish people. They gave up eating and cried out loud, and many of them lay down on rough cloth and ashes to show how sad they were.

NKJV

¹When Mordecai learned all that had happened, he tore his clothes and put on sackcloth and ashes, and went out into the midst of the city. He cried out with a loud and bitter cry. ²He went as far as the front of the king's gate, for no one might enter the king's gate clothed with sackcloth. ³And in every province where the king's command and decree arrived, there was great mourning among the Jews, with fasting, weeping, and wailing; and many lay in sackcloth and ashes.

⁴So Esther's maids and eunuchs came and

NCV

[4]When Esther's servant girls and eunuchs came to her and told her about Mordecai, she was very upset and afraid. She sent clothes for Mordecai to put on instead of the rough cloth, but he would not wear them. [5]Then Esther called for Hathach, one of the king's eunuchs chosen by the king to serve her. Esther ordered him to find out what was bothering Mordecai and why.

[6]So Hathach went to Mordecai, who was in the city square in front of the king's gate. [7]Mordecai told Hathach everything that had happened to him, and he told Hathach about the amount of money Haman had promised to pay into the king's treasury for the killing of the Jewish people. [8]Mordecai also gave him a copy of the order to kill the Jewish people, which had been given in Susa. He wanted Hathach to show it to Esther and to tell her about it. And Mordecai told him to order Esther to go into the king's presence to beg for mercy and to plead with him for her people.

[9]Hathach went back and reported to Esther everything Mordecai had said. [10]Then Esther told Hathach to tell Mordecai, [11]"All the royal officers and people of the royal states know that no man or woman may go to the king in the inner courtyard without being called. There is only one law about this: Anyone who enters must be put to death unless the king holds out his gold scepter. Then that person may live. And I have not been called to go to the king for thirty days."

[12]Esther's message was given to Mordecai. [13]Then Mordecai sent back word to Esther: "Just because you live in the king's palace, don't think

NKJV

told her, and the queen was deeply distressed. Then she sent garments to clothe Mordecai and take his sackcloth away from him, but he would not accept them. [5]Then Esther called Hathach, one of the king's eunuchs whom he had appointed to attend her, and she gave him a command concerning Mordecai, to learn what and why this was. [6]So Hathach went out to Mordecai in the city square that was in front of the king's gate. [7]And Mordecai told him all that had happened to him, and the sum of money that Haman had promised to pay into the king's treasuries to destroy the Jews. [8]He also gave him a copy of the written decree for their destruction, which was given at Shushan, that he might show it to Esther and explain it to her, and that he might command her to go in to the king to make supplication to him and plead before him for her people. [9]So Hathach returned and told Esther the words of Mordecai.

[10]Then Esther spoke to Hathach, and gave him a command for Mordecai: [11]"All the king's servants and the people of the king's provinces know that any man or woman who goes into the inner court to the king, who has not been called, he has but one law: put all to death, except the one to whom the king holds out the golden scepter, that he may live. Yet I myself have not been called to go in to the king these thirty days." [12]So they told Mordecai Esther's words.

[13]And Mordecai told them to answer Esther: "Do not think in your heart that you will escape in the king's palace any more than all the other Jews. [14]For if you remain completely silent at this time, relief and deliverance will arise for

NCV

that out of all the Jewish people you alone will escape. ¹⁴If you keep quiet at this time, someone else will help and save the Jewish people, but you and your father's family will all die. And who knows, you may have been chosen queen for just such a time as this."

¹⁵Then Esther sent this answer to Mordecai: ¹⁶"Go and get all the Jewish people in Susa together. For my sake, give up eating; do not eat or drink for three days, night and day. I and my servant girls will also give up eating. Then I will go to the king, even though it is against the law, and if I die, I die."

¹⁷So Mordecai went away and did everything Esther had told him to do.

NKJV

the Jews from another place, but you and your father's house will perish. Yet who knows whether you have come to the kingdom for such a time as this?"

¹⁵Then Esther told them to reply to Mordecai: ¹⁶"Go, gather all the Jews who are present in Shushan, and fast for me; neither eat nor drink for three days, night or day. My maids and I will fast likewise. And so I will go to the king, which is against the law; and if I perish, I perish!"

¹⁷So Mordecai went his way and did according to all that Esther commanded him.

DISCOVERY

Explore the Bible reading by discussing these questions.

2. How did Mordecai and his people show their sadness?

_____

_____

_____

3. How did Esther find out about her people's situation?

_____

_____

_____

4. Why did Mordecai want Esther to approach the king?

_____

_____

5. What did Esther ask Mordecai to do?

_____

_____

6. What risk was Esther willing to take?

_____

_____

_____

INSPIRATION

Here is an uplifting thought from the *Inspirational Study Bible.*

All of us at times find ourselves and our futures seemingly in the hands of other people. Their decisions or their actions determine whether we get a good grade or a poor one, whether we are promoted or fired, whether our careers blossom or fold. I am not overlooking our own responsibility in these situations, but all of us know that even when we have, so to speak, done our best, we are still dependent upon the favor or frown of that teacher or boss or commanding officer. We are, from a human point of view, often at the mercy of other people and their decisions or actions. . . .

Can we trust God that He can and will work in the heart of that individual to bring about His plan for us? Or consider the instance when someone is out to harm us, to ruin our reputation, or jeopardize our career: Can we trust God to intervene in the heart of that person so that he does not carry out his evil intent? According to the Bible, the answer in both instances is yes. We can trust God.

(from *Trusting God*
by Jerry Bridges)

RESPONSE

Use these questions to share more deeply with each other.

7. What does Esther's decision tell us about the quality of her character?

_____

_____

_____

8. Why was Esther willing to risk her life for her people?

_____

_____

_____

9. How did Esther demonstrate her trust in God?

_____

_____

_____

PRAYER

Father, thank you for helping us when we need to make difficult decisions. We are grateful that you don't turn your back when we need you. Give us wisdom to recognize our responsibility to do what is right, and give us the courage to do it.

JOURNALING

Take a few moments and record your personal insights from this lesson.

In what area of my life do I need to do what's right and trust God with the outcome?

ADDITIONAL QUESTIONS

10. In what ways do we try to hold on to our problems?

_____

_____

_____

11. Why is it important to trust God to help us instead of trying to solve our problems by ourselves?

_____

_____

_____

12. How can you depend on God to help you with a current problem?

_____

_____

_____

For more Bible passages on responsibility, see Genesis 22:1–19; Jonah 1:1–3:5; Matthew 26:36–50; 27:32–55.

To complete the book of Esther during this twelve-part study, read Esther 4:1–17.

ADDITIONAL THOUGHTS

LESSON EIGHT

COURAGE

REFLECTION

Begin your study with thoughts on this question.

1. Think of a challenging situation you faced recently. How did you respond to the challenge?

_____

_____

_____

BIBLE READING

Read Esther 5:1–8 from the NCV or the NKJV.

NCV

¹On the third day Esther put on her royal robes and stood in the inner courtyard of the king's palace, facing the king's hall. The king was sitting on his royal throne in the hall, facing the doorway. ²When the king saw Queen Esther standing in the courtyard, he was pleased. He held out to her the gold scepter that was in his hand, so Esther went forward and touched the end of it.

³The king asked, "What is it, Queen Esther? What do you want to ask me? I will give you as much as half of my kingdom."

NKJV

¹Now it happened on the third day that Esther put on her royal robes and stood in the inner court of the king's palace, across from the king's house, while the king sat on his royal throne in the royal house, facing the entrance of the house. ²So it was, when the king saw Queen Esther standing in the court, that she found favor in his sight, and the king held out to Esther the golden scepter that was in his hand. Then Esther went near and touched the top of the scepter.

³And the king said to her, "What do you

NCV

⁴Esther answered, "My king, if it pleases you, come today with Haman to a banquet that I have prepared for him."

⁵Then the king said, "Bring Haman quickly so we may do what Esther asks."

So the king and Haman went to the banquet Esther had prepared for them. ⁶As they were drinking wine, the king said to Esther, "Now, what are you asking for? I will give it to you. What is it you want? I will give you as much as half of my kingdom."

⁷Esther answered, "This is what I want and what I ask for. ⁸My king, if you are pleased with me and if it pleases you, give me what I ask for and do what I want. Come with Haman tomorrow to the banquet I will prepare for you. Then I will answer your question about what I want."

NKJV

wish, Queen Esther? What is your request? It shall be given to you—up to half the kingdom!"

⁴So Esther answered, "If it pleases the king, let the king and Haman come today to the banquet that I have prepared for him."

⁵Then the king said, "Bring Haman quickly, that he may do as Esther has said." So the king and Haman went to the banquet that Esther had prepared.

⁶At the banquet of wine the king said to Esther, "What is your petition? It shall be granted you. What is your request, up to half the kingdom? It shall be done!"

⁷Then Esther answered and said, "My petition and request is this: ⁸If I have found favor in the sight of the king, and if it pleases the king to grant my petition and fulfill my request, then let the king and Haman come to the banquet which I will prepare for them, and tomorrow I will do as the king has said."

DISCOVERY

Explore the Bible reading by discussing these questions.

2. What did Esther do to meet the king?

_____

_____

_____

3. In what ways did the king show his approval for Esther?

_____

_____

_____

4. What did Esther request of the king?

_____

_____

_____

5. How did Esther show that she believed the king would accept her invitation?

_____

_____

_____

6. What was Esther's strategy for pleasing the king?

_____

_____

_____

INSPIRATION

Here is an uplifting thought from the *Inspirational Study Bible*.

[Courage] is the power to do well when the air is turbulent and the going gets tough. It is having the character to do well when things are tempting, when things are painful. It is easy to be a mother when a baby is cooing and gurgling over breakfast; it takes courage to be a mother when the child suffers from a terrible and incurable handicap. Courage is the power to do well in the face of a threat—to your life, to your security, to your future, to the things you hold dear.

(from "Basic Moral Characteristics"
in *Practical Christianity* by Lewis Smedes)

RESPONSE

Use these questions to share more deeply with each other.

7. What do Esther's actions reveal about her faith in God?

_____

_____

_____

_____

8. How does Esther serve as an example to believers today?

_____

_____

_____

_____

9. How did God honor Esther's faith and courage?

_____

_____

_____

PRAYER

Father, we may appear calm on the outside, but you know our hidden anxieties. We're afraid of being alone. We're afraid of being jobless. We're afraid of pain. Father, we offer these fears to you and ask you, the One who knows no fear, to give us courage to face our challenges.

JOURNALING

Take a few moments to record your personal insights from this lesson.

How can I face future challenges courageously?

ADDITIONAL QUESTIONS

10. What is keeping you from living courageously? How can you overcome those obstacles?

_____

_____

_____

11. Who is an example of courage to you? How can you follow that person's example?

_____

_____

_____

12. In what area of your life do you need God's help to demonstrate courage?

_____

_____

_____

For more Bible passages on courage, see Joshua 1:6–9; Psalm 27:14; Acts 4:1–13; 5:17–32; 20:22–24.

To complete the book of Esther during this twelve-part study, read Esther 5:1–8.

ADDITIONAL THOUGHTS

LESSON NINE

PRIDE

REFLECTION

Begin your study with thoughts on this question.

1. What is the difference between arrogance and being proud of someone or something?

_____

_____

_____

BIBLE READING

Read Esther 5:9–14 from the NCV or the NKJV.

NCV

⁹Haman left the king's palace that day happy and content. But when he saw Mordecai at the king's gate and saw that Mordecai did not stand up or tremble with fear before him, Haman became very angry with Mordecai. ¹⁰But he controlled his anger and went home.

Then Haman called together his friends and his wife, Zeresh. ¹¹He told them how wealthy he was and how many sons he had. He also told them all the ways the king had honored him and how the king had placed him higher than his important men and his royal officers. ¹²He

NKJV

⁹So Haman went out that day joyful and with a glad heart; but when Haman saw Mordecai in the king's gate, and that he did not stand or tremble before him, he was filled with indignation against Mordecai. ¹⁰Nevertheless Haman restrained himself and went home, and he sent and called for his friends and his wife Zeresh. ¹¹Then Haman told them of his great riches, the multitude of his children, everything in which the king had promoted him, and how he had advanced him above the officials and servants of the king.

NCV

also said, "I'm the only person Queen Esther invited to come with the king to the banquet she gave. And tomorrow also the queen has asked me to be her guest with the king. ¹³But all this does not really make me happy when I see that Jew Mordecai sitting at the king's gate."

¹⁴Then Haman's wife, Zeresh, and all his friends said, "Have a seventy-five foot platform built, and in the morning ask the king to have Mordecai hanged on it. Then go to the banquet with the king and be happy." Haman liked this suggestion, so he ordered the platform to be built.

NKJV

¹²Moreover Haman said, "Besides, Queen Esther invited no one but me to come in with the king to the banquet that she prepared; and tomorrow I am again invited by her, along with the king. ¹³Yet all this avails me nothing, so long as I see Mordecai the Jew sitting at the king's gate."

¹⁴Then his wife Zeresh and all his friends said to him, "Let a gallows be made, fifty cubits high, and in the morning suggest to the king that Mordecai be hanged on it; then go merrily with the king to the banquet."

And the thing pleased Haman; so he had the gallows made.

DISCOVERY

Explore the Bible reading by discussing these questions.

2. What was Haman proud of?

_____

_____

_____

3. How did Haman display his pride?

_____

_____

_____

4. What ruined Haman's happiness?

_____

_____

_____

5. How did Haman's family and friends help feed his arrogance?

_____

_____

_____

6. Haman was at the height of his career. Why was he so preoccupied with Mordecai's actions?

_____

_____

_____

INSPIRATION

Here is an uplifting thought from the *Inspirational Study Bible.*

Do not be ashamed to serve others because of your love for Jesus Christ, or to appear poor in the world's eyes.

Do not count on your own strength; trust God. Do what you can, and God will supply the difference. . . .

Take glory neither in money, if you have some, nor in influential friends, but in God who gives you everything and above all wants to give you himself.

Avoid boasting about the size or beauty of your body, which a little illness can disfigure or destroy.

Have no pride in your native wit and talent; that would displease God who gave you every good thing that you naturally possess.

Reject the thought that you are better than anyone else. If you think such haughty thoughts, God (who knows what is in you) will consider you worse than they.

Pride about our good deeds is pointless. God has his own ideas regarding what is good and he does not always agree with us. If there is anything good about you, believe better things of others. This will keep you humble.

It will not hurt you at all to consider yourself less righteous than others, but it will be disastrous for you to consider yourself better than even one person.

The humble are always at peace; the proud are often envious and angry.

(from *The Imitation of Christ* by Thomas à Kempis)

RESPONSE

Use these questions to share more deeply with each other.

7. Why did Haman become angry when Mordecai would not bow down to him?

_____

_____

_____

8. Haman's pride was obvious. How can pride be a subtle sin?

_____

_____

_____

9. How can someone stay humble despite having success in life?

_____

_____

_____

PRAYER

Dear Lord, so often we are focused on our own selves, and we forget that all good things come from you. Thank you for blessing us in so many ways. Give us vision to see and remove the pride in our lives so we will be humble in your sight.

JOURNALING

Take a few moments to record your personal insights from this lesson.

How can I feel good about my accomplishments and yet give the glory to God?

ADDITIONAL QUESTIONS

10. When others boast of their accomplishments, how do you react?

_____

_____

_____

11. Think about your recent attitudes and actions. What evidence of pride do you see?

_____

_____

_____

12. How can you work on eliminating pride from your heart?

_____

_____

_____

For more Bible passages on pride, see Mark 9:34; Luke 18:11–14.

To complete the book of Esther during this twelve-part study, read Esther 5:9–14.

ADDITIONAL THOUGHTS

LESSON TEN

EARNING REWARDS

REFLECTION

Begin your study with thoughts on this question.

1. Think of a time when you received recognition for doing something good. How did you respond?

_____

_____

_____

BIBLE READING

Read Esther 6:1–12 from the NCV or the NKJV.

N C V

¹That same night the king could not sleep. So he gave an order for the daily court record to be brought in and read to him. ²It was found recorded that Mordecai had warned the king about Bigthana and Teresh, two of the king's officers who guarded the doorway and who had planned to kill the king.

N K J V

¹That night the king could not sleep. So one was commanded to bring the book of the records of the chronicles; and they were read before the king. ²And it was found written that Mordecai had told of Bigthana and Teresh, two of the king's eunuchs, the doorkeepers who had sought to lay hands on King Ahasuerus. ³Then

NCV

[3]The king asked, "What honor and reward have been given to Mordecai for this?"

The king's personal servants answered, "Nothing has been done for Mordecai."

[4]The king said, "Who is in the courtyard?" Now Haman had just entered the outer court of the king's palace. He had come to ask the king about hanging Mordecai on the platform he had prepared.

[5]The king's personal servants said, "Haman is standing in the courtyard."

The king said, "Bring him in."

[6]So Haman came in. And the king asked him, "What should be done for a man whom the king wants very much to honor?"

And Haman thought to himself, "Whom would the king want to honor more than me?" [7]So he answered the king, "This is what you could do for the man you want very much to honor. [8]Have the servants bring a royal robe that the king himself has worn. And also bring a horse with a royal crown on its head, a horse that the king himself has ridden. [9]Let the robe and the horse be given to one of the king's most important men. Let the servants put the robe on the man the king wants to honor, and let them lead him on the horse through the city streets. As they are leading him, let them announce: 'This is what is done for the man whom the king wants to honor!'"

[10]The king commanded Haman, "Go quickly. Take the robe and the horse just as you have said, and do all this for Mordecai the Jew who sits at the king's gate. Do not leave out anything you have suggested."

[11]So Haman took the robe and the horse,

NKJV

the king said, "What honor or dignity has been bestowed on Mordecai for this?"

And the king's servants who attended him said, "Nothing has been done for him."

[4]So the king said, "Who is in the court?" Now Haman had just entered the outer court of the king's palace to suggest that the king hang Mordecai on the gallows that he had prepared for him.

[5]The king's servants said to him, "Haman is there, standing in the court."

And the king said, "Let him come in."

[6]So Haman came in, and the king asked him, "What shall be done for the man whom the king delights to honor?"

Now Haman thought in his heart, "Whom would the king delight to honor more than me?" [7]And Haman answered the king, "For the man whom the king delights to honor, [8]let a royal robe be brought which the king has worn, and a horse on which the king has ridden, which has a royal crest placed on its head. [9]Then let this robe and horse be delivered to the hand of one of the king's most noble princes, that he may array the man whom the king delights to honor. Then parade him on horseback through the city square, and proclaim before him: 'Thus shall it be done to the man whom the king delights to honor!'"

[10]Then the king said to Haman, "Hurry, take the robe and the horse, as you have suggested, and do so for Mordecai the Jew who sits within the king's gate! Leave nothing undone of all that you have spoken."

[11]So Haman took the robe and the horse, arrayed Mordecai and led him on horseback

NCV

and he put the robe on Mordecai. Then he led him on horseback through the city streets, announcing before Mordecai: "This is what is done for the man whom the king wants to honor!"

[12]Then Mordecai returned to the king's gate, but Haman hurried home with his head covered, because he was embarrassed and ashamed.

NKJV

through the city square, and proclaimed before him, "Thus shall it be done to the man whom the king delights to honor!"

[12]Afterward Mordecai went back to the king's gate. But Haman hurried to his house, mourning and with his head covered.

DISCOVERY

Explore the Bible reading by discussing these questions.

2. What had Mordecai done to deserve recognition and reward?

_____

_____

_____

3. How did the king find out about Mordecai's actions?

_____

_____

_____

4. How was Mordecai's reward determined?

_____

_____

_____

5. In what ways was Mordecai honored?

_____

_____

_____

6. Why did Haman assume that the king wanted to honor him?

_____

_____

_____

INSPIRATION

Here's an uplifting thought from the *Inspirational Study Bible.*

We should never take any blessing for granted, but accept everything as a gift from the Father of Lights. Whole days may be spent occasionally in the holy practice of being thankful. We should write on a tablet one by one the things for which we are grateful to God and to our fellow men. And a constant return to this thought during the day as our minds get free will serve to fix the habit in our hearts. . . .

In trying to count our many blessings the difficulty is not to find things to count, but to find time to enumerate them all. Personally I have gotten great help from the practice of talking over with God the many kindnesses I have received from my fellow men. To my parents I owe my life and my upbringing. To my teachers I owe that patient line-upon-line instruction that took me when I was a young, ignorant pagan and enabled me to read and write. To the patriots and statesmen of the past I owe the liberties I now enjoy. To numerous and unknown soldiers who shed their blood to keep our country free I owe a debt I can never pay. And I please God and enlarge my own heart when I remind the Lord that I am grateful for them. For every man and woman of every race and nationality who may have contributed anything to my peace and welfare I am grateful, and I shall not let God forget that I am.

(from *The Root of the Righteouss* by A. W. Tozer)

RESPONSE

Use these questions to share more deeply with each other.

7. How do you think Mordecai felt about not being recognized for saving the king?

_____

_____

_____

8. Have you ever done a good deed that went unnoticed? How did you respond?

_____

_____

_____

9. Why is it important to reward and recognize those who do good deeds?

_____

_____

_____

PRAYER

Holy Father, you are so good to us, and often you work through others to show us that goodness, but we do not recognize it. Open our hearts and our eyes to see the kindness of others so we can thank them and praise you.

JOURNALING

Take a few moments to record your personal insights from this lesson.

How can I thank someone who has been good to me?

ADDITIONAL QUESTIONS

10. How can we cultivate a spirit of thankfulness?

_____

_____

_____

11. List some of the good gifts God has given to you.

_____

_____

_____

12. How can you encourage a friend to praise God for his blessings?

_____

_____

_____

For more Bible passages on honoring good deeds, see 2 Chronicles 15:7;
Ezra 7:11–28; Matthew 6:1–4.

To complete the book of Esther during this twelve-part study, read Esther 6:1–14.

ADDITIONAL THOUGHTS

LESSON ELEVEN

JUSTICE ARRIVES

REFLECTION

Begin your study with thoughts on this question.

1. People handle their anger in different ways. In what ways have you seen people deal with their anger?

_____

_____

_____

BIBLE READING

Read Esther 7:1–10 from the NCV or the NKJV.

N C V

¹So the king and Haman went in to eat with Queen Esther. ²As they were drinking wine on the second day, the king asked Esther again, "What are you asking for? I will give it to you. What is it you want? I will give you as much as half of my kingdom."

³Then Queen Esther answered, "My king, if you are pleased with me, and if it pleases you, let me live. This is what I ask. And let my people live, too. This is what I want. ⁴My people and I

N K J V

¹So the king and Haman went to dine with Queen Esther. ²And on the second day, at the banquet of wine, the king again said to Esther, "What is your petition, Queen Esther? It shall be granted you. And what is your request, up to half the kingdom? It shall be done!"

³Then Queen Esther answered and said, "If I have found favor in your sight, O king, and if it pleases the king, let my life be given me at my petition, and my people at my request. ⁴For we

have been sold to be destroyed, to be killed and completely wiped out. If we had been sold as male and female slaves, I would have kept quiet, because that would not be enough of a problem to bother the king."

⁵Then King Xerxes asked Queen Esther, "Who is he, and where is he? Who has done such a thing?"

⁶Esther said, "Our enemy and foe is this wicked Haman!"

Then Haman was filled with terror before the king and queen. ⁷The king was very angry, so he got up, left his wine, and went out into the palace garden. But Haman stayed inside to beg Queen Esther to save his life. He could see that the king had already decided to kill him.

⁸When the king returned from the palace garden to the banquet hall, he saw Haman falling on the couch where Esther was lying. The king said, "Will he even attack the queen while I am in the house?"

As soon as the king said that, servants came in and covered Haman's face. ⁹Harbona, one of the eunuchs there serving the king, said, "Look, a seventy-five foot platform stands near Haman's house. This is the one Haman had prepared for Mordecai, who gave the warning that saved the king."

The king said, "Hang Haman on it!" ¹⁰So they hanged Haman on the platform he had prepared for Mordecai. Then the king was not so angry anymore.

have been sold, my people and I, to be destroyed, to be killed, and to be annihilated. Had we been sold as male and female slaves, I would have held my tongue, although the enemy could never compensate for the king's loss."

⁵So King Ahasuerus answered and said to Queen Esther, "Who is he, and where is he, who would dare presume in his heart to do such a thing?"

⁶And Esther said, "The adversary and enemy is this wicked Haman!"

So Haman was terrified before the king and queen.

⁷Then the king arose in his wrath from the banquet of wine and went into the palace garden; but Haman stood before Queen Esther, pleading for his life, for he saw that evil was determined against him by the king. ⁸When the king returned from the palace garden to the place of the banquet of wine, Haman had fallen across the couch where Esther was. Then the king said, "Will he also assault the queen while I am in the house?"

As the word left the king's mouth, they covered Haman's face. ⁹Now Harbonah, one of the eunuchs, said to the king, "Look! The gallows, fifty cubits high, which Haman made for Mordecai, who spoke good on the king's behalf, is standing at the house of Haman."

Then the king said, "Hang him on it!"

¹⁰So they hanged Haman on the gallows that he had prepared for Mordecai. Then the king's wrath subsided.

DISCOVERY

Explore the Bible reading by discussing these questions.

2. How did the king encourage Esther to ask for what she wanted?

_____

_____

_____

3. How is Esther's humility and courage revealed in the way she presented her request to the king?

_____

_____

_____

4. How did the king handle his anger after Esther's revelation?

_____

_____

_____

5. What was Haman's response to Esther's accusations?

_____

_____

_____

6. How did Esther respond honorably to her conflict with Haman?

_____

_____

_____

INSPIRATION

Here is an uplifting thought from the *Inspirational Study Bible*.

If you find yourself dealing with people who are not playing by the biblical rules, who are underhanded, deceptive, dishonest, and self-serving, can you learn to see the advantage you have over them? In refusing to use their tactics and choosing to abide by biblical principles, you are under God's protection, and He has promised to honor you and to prosper you.

A few years ago, while in the process of purchasing a newly built home, I found myself engaged in a conflict with one of the employees of the building firm. She was arrogant, rude, and terribly disrespectful to me, the customer. I responded as I knew a businessperson should: I was assertive, refused to talk to her, went to a higher authority, and demanded my rights. . . .

Instead of raising my voice and demanding my rights, I could have been just as assertive by calmly repeating my concerns, refusing to allow the conversation to deteriorate to that low level. I could have been kind and polite; I could have stopped and quickly prayed for the woman; I could have thought about what bitterness and anger there was inside her to cause her to behave the way she did and allowed God to give me compassion for her. I could have done all that, but I missed the opportunity because I was too concerned with the way she was treating me.

I'm not suggesting we become doormats, but we can control our reactions and respond in a Christlike manner, we actually have the advantage over the other person. When we take the world's way out, we often lose our Christian advantage, not to mention our testimony for Christ.

When our business dealings are guided by biblical principles, it gives us a great advantage.

(from *Workday Meditations*
by Mary Whelchel)

RESPONSE

Use these questions to share more deeply with each other.

7. What principles can we glean from this passage about resolving conflicts?

_____

_____

_____

8. Have you recently experienced a situation that needed a Christlike response? Explain.

_____

_____

_____

9. When have you applied a biblical principle to resolving a problem with a coworker or friend? What was the result?

_____

_____

_____

PRAYER

Dear Father, sometimes in our anger and frustration we sin. Thank you for forgiving us so we do not live burdened and shackled by failures. Please help us to respond to others in a way that glorifies you.

JOURNALING

Take a few moments to record your personal insights from this lesson.

How can I make godly responses a habit in my life?

ADDITIONAL QUESTIONS

10. What are some different ways of handling anger?

_____

_____

_____

11. How can diffusing your anger work to your advantage?

_____

_____

_____

12. What practical steps can you take to control your anger?

_____

_____

_____

For more Bible passages on having a Christlike response, see Genesis 50:19–21; Matthew 5:43–48; Romans 12:9–17; Galatians 5:13–15; Ephesians 4:26.

To complete the book of Esther during this twelve-part study, read Esther 7:1–10.

ADDITIONAL THOUGHTS

LESSON TWELVE

FAITHFULNESS

REFLECTION

Begin your study with thoughts on this question.

1. What sacrifices would you be willing to make for someone you love?

_____

_____

_____

BIBLE READING

Read Esther 8:1–16 from the NCV or the NKJV.

NCV

¹That same day King Xerxes gave Queen Esther everything Haman, the enemy of the Jewish people, had left when he died. And Mordecai came in to see the king, because Esther had told the king how he was related to her. ²Then the king took off his signet ring that he had taken back from Haman, and he gave it to Mordecai. Esther put Mordecai in charge of everything Haman left when he died.

³Once again Esther spoke to the king. She fell

NKJV

¹On that day King Ahasuerus gave Queen Esther the house of Haman, the enemy of the Jews. And Mordecai came before the king, for Esther had told how he was related to her. ²So the king took off his signet ring, which he had taken from Haman, and gave it to Mordecai; and Esther appointed Mordecai over the house of Haman.

³Now Esther spoke again to the king, fell down at his feet, and implored him with tears

NCV

at the king's feet and cried and begged him to stop the evil plan that Haman the Agagite had planned against the Jews. ⁴The king held out the gold scepter to Esther. So Esther got up and stood in front of him.

⁵She said, "My king, if you are pleased with me, and if it pleases you to do this, if you think it is the right thing to do, and if you are happy with me, let an order be written to cancel the letters Haman wrote. Haman the Agagite sent messages to destroy all the Jewish people in all of your kingdom. ⁶I could not stand to see that terrible thing happen to my people. I could not stand to see my family killed."

⁷King Xerxes answered Queen Esther and Mordecai the Jew, "Because Haman was against the Jewish people, I have given his things to Esther, and my soldiers have hanged him. ⁸Now, in the king's name, write another order to the Jewish people as it seems best to you. Then seal the order with the king's signet ring, because no letter written in the king's name and sealed with his signet ring can be canceled."

⁹At that time the king's secretaries were called. This was the twenty-third day of the third month, which is Sivan. The secretaries wrote out all of Mordecai's orders to the Jews, to the governors, to the captains of the soldiers in each state, and to the important men of the one hundred twenty-seven states that reached from India to Cush. They wrote in the writing of each state and in the language of each people. They also wrote to the Jewish people in their own writing and language. ¹⁰Mordecai wrote orders in the name of King Xerxes and sealed the letters with the king's signet ring.

NKJV

to counteract the evil of Haman the Agagite, and the scheme which he had devised against the Jews. ⁴And the king held out the golden scepter toward Esther. So Esther arose and stood before the king, ⁵and said, "If it pleases the king, and if I have found favor in his sight and the thing seems right to the king and I am pleasing in his eyes, let it be written to revoke the letters devised by Haman, the son of Hammedatha the Agagite, which he wrote to annihilate the Jews who are in all the king's provinces. ⁶For how can I endure to see the evil that will come to my people? Or how can I endure to see the destruction of my countrymen?"

⁷Then King Ahasuerus said to Queen Esther and Mordecai the Jew, "Indeed, I have given Esther the house of Haman, and they have hanged him on the gallows because he tried to lay his hand on the Jews. ⁸You yourselves write a decree concerning the Jews, as you please, in the king's name, and seal it with the king's signet ring; for whatever is written in the king's name and sealed with the king's signet ring no one can revoke."

⁹So the king's scribes were called at that time, in the third month, which is the month of Sivan, on the twenty-third day; and it was written, according to all that Mordecai commanded, to the Jews, the satraps, the governors, and the princes of the provinces from India to Ethiopia, one hundred and twenty-seven provinces in all, to every province in its own script, to every people in their own language, and to the Jews in their own script and language. ¹⁰And he wrote in the name of King Ahasuerus,

NCV

Then he sent the king's orders by messengers on fast horses, horses that were raised just for the king.

[11]These were the king's orders: The Jewish people in every city have the right to gather together to protect themselves. They may destroy, kill, and completely wipe out the army of any state or people who attack them. And they are to do the same to the women and children of that army. They may also take by force the property of their enemies. [12]The one day set for the Jewish people to do this in all the empire of King Xerxes was the thirteenth day of the twelfth month, the month of Adar. [13]A copy of the king's order was to be sent out as a law in every state. It was to be made known to the people of every nation living in the kingdom so the Jewish people would be ready on that set day to strike back at their enemies.

[14]The messengers hurried out, riding on the royal horses, because the king commanded those messengers to hurry. And the order was also given in the palace at Susa.

[15]Mordecai left the king's presence wearing royal clothes of blue and white and a large gold crown. He also had a purple robe made of the best linen. And the people of Susa shouted for joy. [16]It was a time of happiness, joy, gladness, and honor for the Jewish people. [17]As the king's order went to every state and city, there was joy and gladness among the Jewish people. In every state and city to which the king's order went, they were having feasts and celebrating. And many people through all the empire became Jews, because they were afraid of the Jewish people.

NKJV

sealed it with the king's signet ring, and sent letters by couriers on horseback, riding on royal horses bred from swift steeds.

[11]By these letters the king permitted the Jews who were in every city to gather together and protect their lives—to destroy, kill, and annihilate all the forces of any people or province that would assault them, both little children and women, and to plunder their possessions, [12]on one day in all the provinces of King Ahasuerus, on the thirteenth day of the twelfth month, which is the month of Adar. [13]A copy of the document was to be issued as a decree in every province and published for all people, so that the Jews would be ready on that day to avenge themselves on their enemies. [14]The couriers who rode on royal horses went out, hastened and pressed on by the king's command. And the decree was issued in Shushan the citadel.

[15]So Mordecai went out from the presence of the king in royal apparel of blue and white, with a great crown of gold and a garment of fine linen and purple; and the city of Shushan rejoiced and was glad. [16]The Jews had light and gladness, joy and honor. [17]And in every province and city, wherever the king's command and decree came, the Jews had joy and gladness, a feast and a holiday. Then many of the people of the land became Jews, because fear of the Jews fell upon them.

DISCOVERY

Explore the Bible reading by discussing these questions.

2. What did Esther beg the king to do?

_____

_____

_____

3. What was the king's response to Esther's pleading?

_____

_____

_____

4. Mordecai now enjoyed great benefits. What were they?

_____

_____

_____

5. What did the king's new orders allow the Jewish people to do?

_____

_____

_____

6. What was the Jewish people's response to the new orders?

_____

_____

_____

INSPIRATION

Here is an uplifting thought from the *Inspirational Study Bible.*

God's power to take the most negative situations and turn them into positive realities worthy of His praise is demonstrated throughout biblical history. There is not a crisis that goes beyond the bounds of God's creative power. Whether the difficulties come from Satan or other people, or are self-inflicted, or are experienced in the process of our obedience, it is the prerogative of God to rearrange, reconstruct, reinterpret, and realign the situation to bring glory and praise to His name. . . . Even Christ's death on the cross was transformed by the power of God into positive results and residual benefits of the redemption that many of us have come to know and enjoy. Since God is just, all that He permits is consistent with His justice. . . . God's justice guarantees that ultimately all that is unfair will be dealt with. We are naive to assume that all of life in its fallen condition is fair and just. It is only safe to realize that God is just and that in His time and in His own way He will deal with both the injustice and those who have been unjust.

(from *The Upside of Down,*
by Joseph Stowell)

RESPONSE

Use these questions to share more deeply with each other.

7. In what ways is God's hand seen throughout this passage?

_____

_____

_____

8. In what ways did Mordecai experience justice?

_____

_____

_____

9. When have you personally seen God turn an unjust situation into good?

_____

_____

_____

PRAYER

Father, it is frustrating when life is not fair, when the unjust seem to be prospering. We struggle when it seems your justice is slow in coming. But you are a just God, and you promise to ultimately deal with all unfairness and injustice in your own time. Help us to trust you with the big picture and to have patience in your timing.

JOURNALING

Take a few moments to record your personal insights from this lesson.

How can I use God's faithfulness to keep a godly perspective on life?

ADDITIONAL QUESTIONS

10. Why is it difficult to trust God when we are treated unjustly?

_____

_____

_____

11. How can we remind ourselves of God's justice when we are surrounded by injustice?

_____

_____

_____

12. In what area of your life do you need to wait patiently for justice to prevail?

_____

_____

_____

For more Bible passages on justice, see Exodus 34:6–7; Deuteronomy 32:4; Psalm 9:16; Micah 6:8; Acts 17:31.

To complete the book of Esther during this twelve-part study, read Esther 8:1–10:3

ADDITIONAL THOUGHTS

ADDITIONAL THOUGHTS

LEADERS' NOTES

LESSON ONE

Question 6: Because Ruth was not from Bethlehem, she would have to adapt to a new culture. Custom, religion, food, and lifestyle were all going to be new to her. She might have been leaving family, such as parents, brothers, and sisters. With this move she was willing to be uncomfortable and to honor her commitment to Naomi.

Question 8: Challenge participants to be honest about their loyalty to others. Challenge each person to rate his or her loyalty on a scale of "not loyal, sometimes loyal, usually loyal, always loyal."

LESSON TWO

Question 6: It was beneficial for a woman to glean in a field where she had found favor with the owner. Women who did not have the favor of the owner could experience disrespect from the men and could be molested.

LESSON THREE

Question 4: By throwing a mantle over a woman, a man would be claiming her as a wife. Ruth, in asking Boaz to throw his skirt over her, was signifying her desire to marry him. Boaz affirmed her and wanted to redeem her. He recognized, though, that there was someone closer in relation who had a greater right to marry her. Boaz provided the man with the opportunity but promised to redeem her if the other man refused. Boaz exercised extreme caution when he urged Ruth to leave early in the morning. By leaving early, no one would see her and wrongly assume sexual misconduct between her and Boaz. Boaz was careful to protect her reputation.

Question 11: Some group members may not consider themselves a risk taker. Encourage them to look back on their lives and share a time when they have risked in some way.

LESSON FOUR

Question 3: Due to the death of Ruth's first husband, someone needed to inherit the land and continue his family name. By marrying Ruth and having a child, Boaz demonstrated respect for Ruth and her first husband.

LESSON FIVE

Question 7: You might discuss what it was like for Mordecai, probably widowed or not married, to adopt and care for a young girl as his own daughter.

Question 8: God uses our experiences to prepare us for what lies ahead. Often it is not until later that we see how God has worked out events and details and prepared us for a situation. Encourage participants to look back at past experiences to see God at work in their lives.

LESSON SIX

Question 4: It is important to note here the degree of Haman's anger. Encourage group members to examine his response in depth.

Question 6: Have your group examine Mordecai's reasons for refusing to bow down to Haman and his ability to stand firm in what he believed.

LESSON SEVEN

Question 8: Mordecai challenged Esther to recognize that she had been made queen for a purpose. Encourage members to look at Esther's moral responsibility and her desire to do what was right.

Question 9: Because Esther was Jewish, we know she believed in God and thus probably interpreted Mordecai's response as meaning that God had a plan for her life and had made her queen for a purpose. Note what she does before she meets the king.

LESSON EIGHT

Question 5: Note that Esther had invited the king and Haman to a banquet that was already prepared.

Question 6: It is obvious that Esther had a plan. Take time to examine her methods and actions.

Question 7: Even though Esther had a strategy, she trusted God to work out the details.

LESSON NINE

Question 7: Haman was extremely proud of himself and his accomplishments. He thought himself important and wanted others to think that as well. When one person did not acknowledge his power and position, he grew furious.

Question 8: Be prepared to share first how pride has been a subtle sin in your life.

LESSON TEN

Question 5: Discuss the irony that during the impending Jewish annihilation, a Jew was being honored.

Question 6: Encourage the group to put themselves in Haman's place to better understand his thoughts and emotions.

LESSON ELEVEN

Question 6: Esther, in her anger with Haman, could have planned revenge on him. She could have used her power as queen to depose him, but she didn't. Examine her actions in this situation.

Question 7: Esther easily could have made her request at the first banquet. Discuss with the group: What was her purpose in waiting until the second banquet?

Question 10: Discuss different ways people handle anger and why. Be sure to discuss how God wants us to handle our anger.

LESSON TWELVE

Question 9: Maybe someone in the group has been treated unfairly by an employer, a co-worker, family member, or friend. Have members share how these situations were handled and the results.

Question 10: We need to be reminded that God is not subject to our timetable. Even though we may not see his justice in our lifetime, his justice guarantees that all unfairness will be dealt with. Biblical history proves that God is consistent in his justice and that all things work together for good to those who love God.

ADDITIONAL NOTES

ADDITIONAL NOTES

ADDITIONAL NOTES

ADDITIONAL NOTES

ADDITIONAL NOTES

ACKNOWLEDGMENTS

à Kempis, Thomas. *The Imitation of Christ*, reprinted in *Christian Classics in Modern English*, copyright 1991 by Bernard Bangley. Used with Permission of Harold Shaw Publishers, Wheaton, Illinois, 60189.

Bridges, Jerry. *Trusting God*, copyright 1988. Permission granted by NavPress. For copies call 1-800-366-7788.

Campolo, Tony. *Who Switched the Price Tags?*, copyright 1986 W Publishing Group, Nashville, TN.

Chambers, Oswald. *My Utmost for His Highest*, copyright 1935 by Dodd Mead and Co., renewed 1963 by the Oswald Chambers Publications Association. Ltd., and is used by permission of Discovery House Publishers, Box 3566, Grand Rapids. MI 49501. All rights reserved.

Lucado, Max. *On the Anvil*, copyright 1985 by Max Lucado. Used by permission of Tyndale House Publishers, Inc. All rights reserved.

Palms, Roger C. *God Guides Your Tomorrows*, copyright 1987, InterVarsity Press.

Smedes, Lewis. "Basic Moral Characteristics" in *Practical Christianity*. Compiled and edited by LaVonne Neff, Ron Beers, Bruce Barton, Linda Taylor, Dave Veerman, and Jim Galvin, copyright 1987 by Youth for Christ/USA. Used by permission of Tyndale House Publishers, Inc. All rights Reserved.

Stowell, Joseph. *The Upside of Down*, copyright 1991, Moody Press.

Swindoll, Charles. *Simple Faith*, copyright 1991, W Publishing Group, Nashville, TN.

Tozer, A. W. *The Root of the Righteous*, copyright 1986, Christian Publications.

Whelchel, Mary. *Workday Meditations*, copyright 1992, Fleming H. Revell Company, a division of Baker Book House Company, Grand Rapids, Michigan.